TULSA CITY-COUNTY LIBRARY

W9-ANO-615

Copyright © 2019 by Aurora Cacciapuoti.

All rights reserved. No part of this book may be reproduced in any form without written permission from the publisher.

Library of Congress Cataloging-in-Publication Data available.

ISBN 978-1-4521-6625-4

Manufactured in China.

Design by Nami Kurita. Cover design and art direction by Alice Seiler.
Typeset in Archer, Heisei Maru Gothic, Meltow, Paqui, and Zooja.

10 9 8 7 6 5 4 3 2

Chronicle Books LLC
680 Second Street
San Francisco, California 94107

Chronicle Books—we see things differently.
Become part of our community at www.chroniclekids.com.

# Let's Learn
# Japanese

## First Words for Everyone

Aurora Cacciapuoti

chronicle books · san francisco

# Introduction

Welcome to *Let's Learn Japanese!*

Imagine having three different alphabets in your language to express yourself. That's what reading and writing in Japanese is like!

The Japanese writing system is made up of two types of syllabic alphabets: hiragana (ひらがな) and katakana (カタカナ). There are also kanji (漢字) characters, which are ideograms adopted from the Chinese. Putting these three types of characters together is called *kanjikanamajiri*.

All three types of characters (hiragana, katakana, and kanji) can be used in combination to write a sentence.

**For example:** 私はレストランに行く。

Watashi wa resutoran ni iku.

I go to the restaurant.

は, に, and く: hiragana
レストラン: katakana
私 and 行: kanji

**Hiragana** is a set of writing symbols composed of 46 base characters, including 5 singular vowels, 40 consonant–vowel unions, and 1 singular consonant. Each character represents a specific sound. Hiragana characters have a more "round" shape and are mainly used for the grammatical elements of sentences.

**Katakana** characters represent the same sounds as hiragana, but they are more "square" in shape and are usually used for words of foreign origin. For example, "computer" is written "コンピューター" (Konpyūtā).

Katakana is used also for scientific words, onomatopoeia (words that are similar to the sounds they refer to, like "boom" or "meow"), and when giving a word extra emphasis.

Hiragana and katakana are both in the kana system.

**If you want to** start studying Japanese, learning these characters by heart is a great place to start. In Japan, children are taught hiragana and katakana first, which is why children's books in Japan are written in kana.

If you don't know how to write a word in kanji, you can use kana and still be understood.

**Kanji** are ideographic symbols adopted from Chinese characters. There are about 50,000 kanji characters in the Japanese language and around 2,000 are commonly used today.

In Japanese schools, students must learn 2,136 kanji that are essential in everyday life. These are called the *jōyō kanji*.

一　十　オ　木

1　　2　　3　　4

The brush strokes that make up each kanji are written in a specific order and direction.

Kanji can have more than one pronunciation.

In this book you will find words written in the Roman alphabet to help you pronounce the word in Japanese. This is called *rōmaji*.

Each word in this book is written in English, kanji (if applicable), followed by the appropriate kana (hiragana and/or katakana), and rōmaji to help with pronunciation:

Cat       - - - -   English

猫         - - - -   Kanji

ねこ       - - - -   Kana

Neko      - - - -   Rōmaji

This book is meant to be an introduction to Japanese as you begin your language-learning journey. In the meantime, enjoy *Let's Learn Japanese*!

Turtle
亀
かめ
Kame

Dog
犬
いぬ
Inu

Cat
猫
ねこ
Neko

Horse
馬
うま
Uma

Elephant
象
ぞう
Zō

Sheep
羊
ひつじ
Hitsuji

Fox
狐
きつね
Kitsune

Cow
牛
うし
Ushi

Bird
鳥
とり
Tori

Fish
魚
さかな
Sakana

Deer
鹿
しか
Shika

Whale
鯨
くじら
Kujira

**Face**
顔
かお
Kao

**Eyebrow**
眉
まゆ
Mayu

**Eye**
目
め
Me

**Neck**
首
くび
Kubi

**Mouth**
口
くち
Kuchi

**Foot**
足
あし
Ashi

Hair
髪
かみ
Kami

Ear
耳
みみ
Mimi

Nose
鼻
はな
Hana

Shoulder
肩
かた
Kata

Hand
手
て
Te

Leg
足
あし
Ashi

### Garlic
大蒜
にんにく
Ninniku

### Soybeans
大豆
だいず
Daizu

### Pumpkin
南瓜
かぼちゃ
Kabocha

### Ginger
生姜
しょうが
Shōga

### Turnip
蕪
かぶ
Kabu

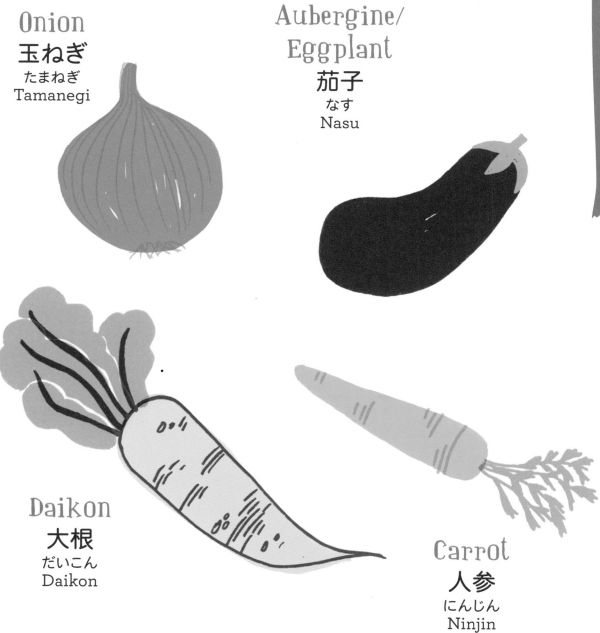

Onion
玉ねぎ
たまねぎ
Tamanegi

Aubergine/
Eggplant
茄子
なす
Nasu

Daikon
大根
だいこん
Daikon

Carrot
人参
にんじん
Ninjin

## Apricot

杏
あんず
Anzu

## Melon
メロン
Meron

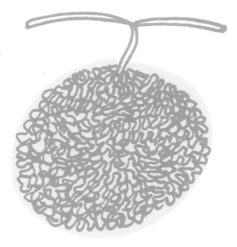

## Apple
林檎
りんご
Ringo

## Banana
バナナ
Banana

## Tangerine
蜜柑
みかん
Mikan

## Strawberry
苺
いちご
Ichigo

**Peach**
桃
もも
Momo

**Cherry**
桜桃
桜んぼ
Sakuranbo

**Watermelon**
西瓜
すいか
Suika

**Plum**
梅
うめ
Ume

**Persimmon**
柿
かき
Kaki

**Pear**
梨
なし
Nashi

## Tofu
豆腐
とうふ
Tōfu

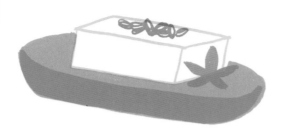

## Sushi
寿司
すし
Sushi

## Raw fish
刺身
さしみ
Sashimi

## Miso soup
味噌汁
みそしる
Misoshiru

## Cooked rice
ご飯
ごはん
Gohan

## Fermented soybeans
納豆
なっとう
Nattō

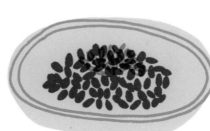

## Soy sauce

醤油
しょうゆ
Shōyu

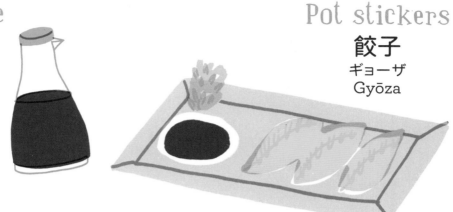

## Pot stickers

餃子
ギョーザ
Gyōza

## Powdered
## green tea

抹茶
まっちゃ
Matcha

## Soy milk

豆乳
とうにゅう
Tōnyū

## Bread

パン
Pan

## Sandwich

サンドイッチ
Sandoitchi

**Gray**
灰色
はいいろ
Haiiro

**Black**
黒
くろ
Kuro

**Purple**
紫
むらさき
Murasaki

**Blue**
青
あお
Ao

**Green**
緑
みどり
Midori

Pink
ピンク
Pinku

White
白
しろ
Shiro

Yellow
黄色
きいろ
Kiiro

Brown
茶色
ちゃいろ
Chaiiro

Red
赤
あか
Aka

Orange
オレンジ
Orenji

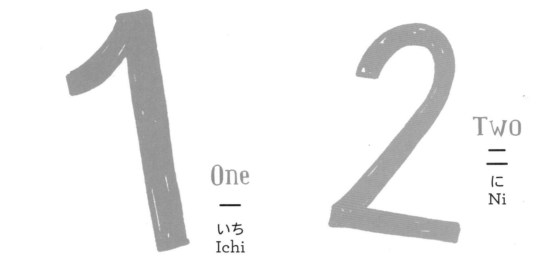

One
一
いち
Ichi

Two
二
に
Ni

Three
三
さん
San

Four
四
よん
Yon

Five
五
ご
Go

6

**Six**
六
ろく
Roku

**Seven**
七
なな
Nana

7

8

**Eight**
八
はち
Hachi

9

**Nine**
九
きゅう
Kyū

10

**Ten**
十
じゅう
Jū

## Festival
祭
まつり
Matsuri

## Japanese inn
旅館
りょかん
Ryokan

## Passport
パスポート
Pasupōto

## Guidebook
ガイドブック
Gaidobukku

## Souvenir
お土産
おみやげ
Omiyage

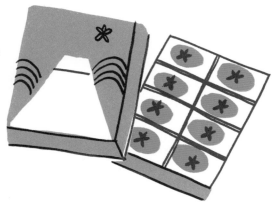

**Baggage**
荷物
にもつ
Nimotsu

**Flight**
便
びん
Bin

**Station**
駅
えき
Eki

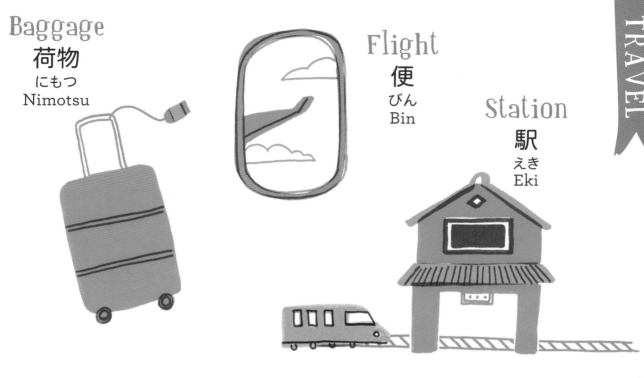

**Map**
地図
ちず
Chizu

**Bathhouse**
銭湯
せんとう
Sentō

## Homework
### 宿題
しゅくだい
Shukudai

## Desk
### 机
つくえ
Tsukue

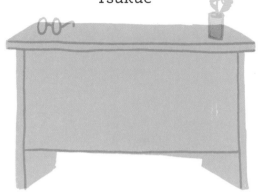

## Library
### 図書館
としょかん
Toshokan

## Uniform
### 制服
せいふく
Seifuku

## Student
### 学生
がくせい
Gakusei

## Classroom
教室
きょうしつ
Kyōshitsu

23 × 7 =

## Lesson
授業
じゅぎょう
Jugyō

## Teacher
先生
せんせい
Sensei

## Book
本
ほん
Hon

## Paper
紙
かみ
Kami

## Pencil
鉛筆
えんぴつ
Enpitsu

## Bookshelf
本棚
ほんだな
Hondana

## Vase
花瓶
かびん
Kabin

## Clock
時計
とけい
Tokei

## Tatami mat
畳
たたみ
Tatami

## Bedroom
寝室
しんしつ
Shinshitsu

## Pillow
枕
まくら
Makura

## Key
鍵
かぎ
Kagi

## Cupboard
戸棚
とだな
Todana

## Door
ドア
Doa

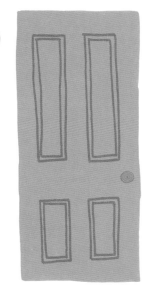

## Window
窓
まど
Mado

## Chair
椅子
いす
Isu

## Kitchen
台所
だいどころ
Daidokoro

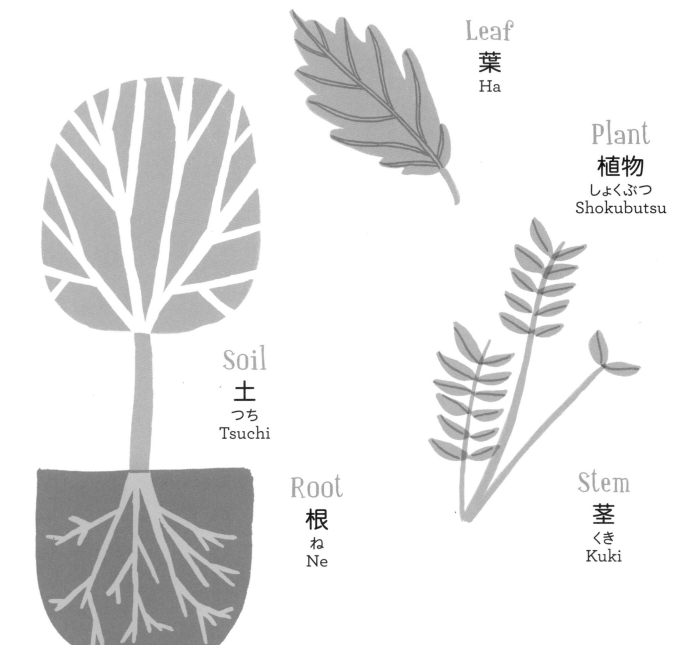

Leaf
葉
Ha

Plant
植物
しょくぶつ
Shokubutsu

Soil
土
つち
Tsuchi

Root
根
ね
Ne

Stem
茎
くき
Kuki

## Seeds
種
たね
Tane

## Insect
虫
むし
Mushi

## Flower
花
はな
Hana

## Grass
草
くさ
Kusa

## Sprout
芽
め
Me

## Gloves
手袋
てぶくろ
Tebukuro

## Sweater
セーター
Sētā

## Socks
靴下
くつした
Kutsushita

## Coat
上着
うわぎ
Uwagi

## Kimono
着物
きもの
Kimono

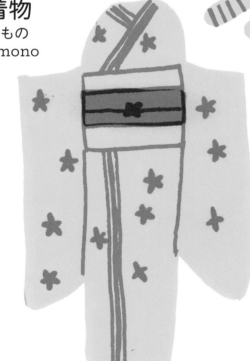

## Shoe
靴
くつ
Kutsu

## Hat
### 帽子
ぼうし
Bōshi

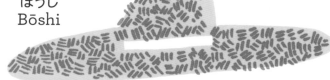

## Eyeglasses
### 眼鏡
めがね
Megane

## Bathing suit
### 水着
みずぎ
Mizugi

## Umbrella
### 傘
かさ
Kasa

## Bag
### 鞄
かばん
Kaban

## Underwear
### 下着
したぎ
Shitagi

Scientist
科学者
かがくしゃ
Kagakusha

Craftsperson
職人
しょくにん
Shokunin

Doctor
医者
いしゃ
Isha

Driver
運転手
うんてんしゅ
Untenshu

Actor
(male)
俳優
はいゆう
Haiyū

Musician
音楽家
おんがくか
Ongakuka

Actor
(female)
女優
じょゆう
Joyū

Writer
作家
さっか
Sakka

Singer
歌手
かしゅ
Kashu

Nurse
(female)
看護婦
かんごふ
Kangofu

Nurse
(male or female)
看護師
かんごし
Kangoshi

Artist
画家
がか
Gaka

Chef
シェフ
Shefu

Photographer
写真家
しゃしんか
Shashinka

## Grandfather
祖父
そふ
Sofu

## Grandmother
祖母
そぼ
Sobo

## Mother
母
はは
Haha

## Uncle
伯父
(older than parent)
叔父
(younger than parent)
おじ
Oji

## Daughter
娘
むすめ
Musume

## Son
息子
むすこ
Musuko

## Father

父
ちち
Chichi

## Aunt

伯母
(older than parent)

叔母
(younger than parent)

おば
Oba

## Sister

姉
(older sister)
あね
Ane

妹
(Younger sister)
いもうと
Imōto

## Brother

兄
(older brother)
あに
Ani

弟
(younger brother)
おとうと
Otōto

## Lake
湖
みずうみ
Mizūmi

## Forest
森
もり
Mori

## Art museum
美術館
びじゅつかん
Bijutsukan

## Mountain
山
やま
Yama

## House
家
いえ
Ie

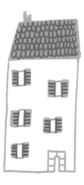

## Town
町
まち
Machi

## Sea
海
うみ
Umi

## Theater
劇場
げきじょう
Gekijō

## River
川
かわ
Kawa

## Desert
砂漠
さばく
Sabaku

## Market
市場
いちば
Ichiba

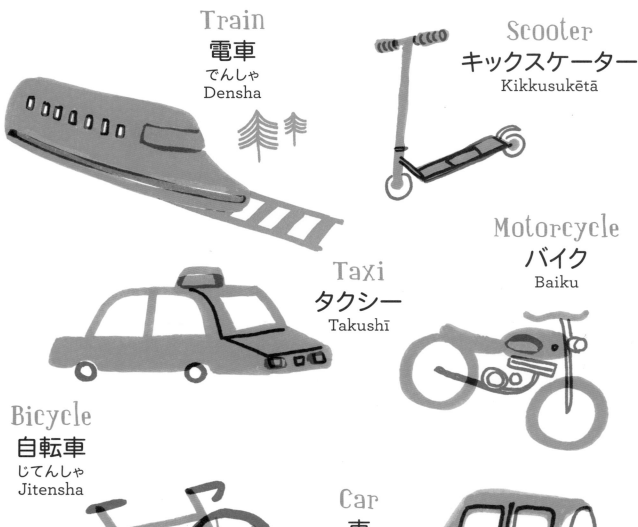

Train
電車
でんしゃ
Densha

Scooter
キックスケーター
Kikkusukētā

Motorcycle
バイク
Baiku

Taxi
タクシー
Takushī

Bicycle
自転車
じてんしゃ
Jitensha

Car
車
くるま
Kuruma

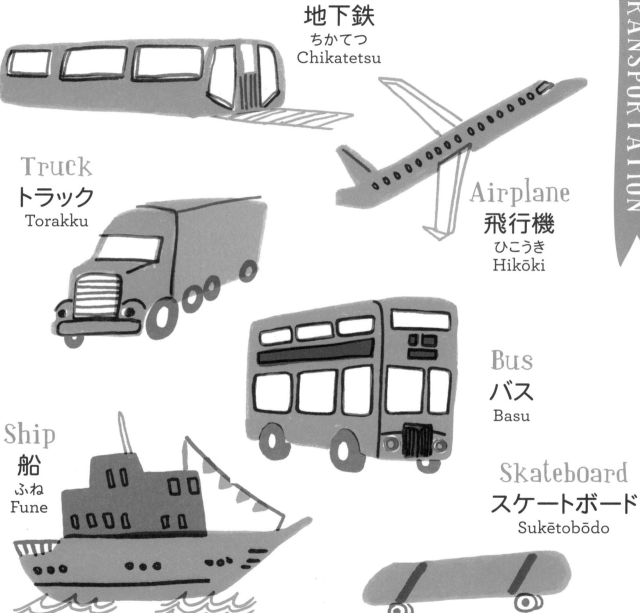

Subway
地下鉄
ちかてつ
Chikatetsu

Truck
トラック
Torakku

Airplane
飛行機
ひこうき
Hikōki

Bus
バス
Basu

Ship
船
ふね
Fune

Skateboard
スケートボード
Sukētobōdo

Cloud
雲
くも
Kumo

Sun
太陽
たいよう
Taiyō

Spring
春
はる
Haru

Rain
雨
あめ
Ame

Summer
夏
なつ
Natsu

Snow
雪
ゆき
Yuki

Autumn
秋
あき
Aki

Fog
霧
きり
Kiri

Wind
風
かぜ
Kaze

Winter
冬
ふゆ
Fuyu

Aurora Cacciapuoti is an author and illustrator of more than a dozen books. She lives in L'Aquila, Italy, with her husband, Armando, and her dog, Yuka.